A Pillar Box Red Publication

in association with

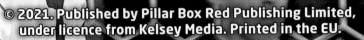

THE BEST FOOTBALL MAGAZINE!

ISBN: 978-1-912456-90-1

Photographs: © Getty Images.

FOOTBALL SKILLS

2022

Written by
Sam Straw

Edited by
Stephen Fishlock

Designed by
Darryl Tooth

CONTENTS

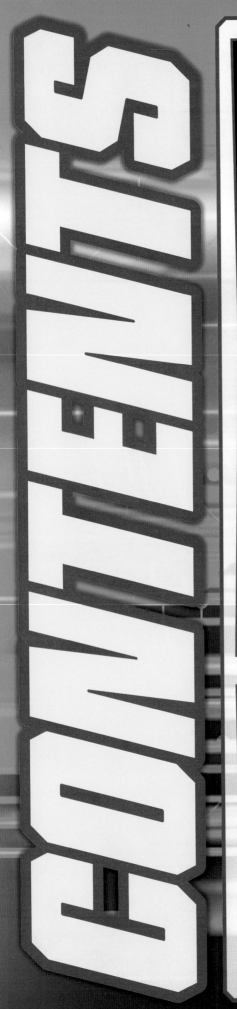

BEN NUTTALL INTERVIEW 46

FIFA SKILLS 14, 22, 36 & 54

WOMEN SKILLERS 58

50
EMILIANO BUENDIA

Club: Aston Villa
Country: Argentina
DOB: 25/12/1996

Buendia helped Norwich win promotion back to the Prem at the first attempt with some epic displays, before sealing a massive transfer to Villa! Not only does the silky skiller have the ability to go on mazy runs, but he also has a steely side to his game that has helped him adapt to the physical nature of footy in England!

CONFIDENCE	DRIBBLING	TRICKS	AGILITY	WEAK FOOT
82	80	81	81	84

49
MATHEUS PEREIRA

Club: Al Hilal
Country: Brazil
DOB: 05/05/1996

The Brazilian midfielder was a big hit in England during his epic two-season spell at West Brom, wowing fans with his wicked tekkers! He always has that piece of magic up his sleeve, which is why following The Baggies' relegation in 2021, mega-rich Saudi giants Al Hilal splashed the cash to snap him up!

CONFIDENCE	DRIBBLING	TRICKS	AGILITY	WEAK FOOT
82	79	78	52	75

48
JACK GREALISH

TOP SKILL!
THE BALL ROLL!

Club: Man. City
Country: England
DOB: 10/09/1995

Man. City's £100-million man has been compared with PSG megastar Lionel Messi because of the way the ball always sticks to his feet! The silky Three Lions baller is one of those players who can control the pace of a game with his balance and amazing control! He even wears child-sized shin pads while playing so that he can control the ball more effectively!

CONFIDENCE	DRIBBLING	TRICKS	AGILITY	WEAK FOOT
85	85	82	85	75

47

EBERECHI EZE

Club: *Crystal Palace*
Country: *England*
DOB: *29/06/1998*

After being a standout player for The Eagles in 2020-21, The Young Lions midfielder was unlucky to be ruled out for so long with a serious injury! He's already scored some memorable goals in the Prem, including running the length of the pitch to net a stunner against Sheffield United at Selhurst Park!

TOP SKILL! THE ROULETTE TURN!

CONFIDENCE	DRIBBLING	TRICKS	AGILITY	WEAK FOOT
82	81	77	80	75

46

CHRISTIAN FUCHS

Club: *Charlotte FC*
Country: *Austria*
DOB: *07/04/1986*

The 6ft 2in defender might've been the last player you were expecting to have top tekkers, but we've exclusively been told by football freestyler Andrew Henderson that the Austrian is an outrageous low-key skiller! He also spends a lot of his spare time playing FIFA, so we reckon EA should give him five-star skills just for a laugh!

CONFIDENCE	DRIBBLING	TRICKS	AGILITY	WEAK FOOT
70	66	76	61	70

45

RICHARLISON

Club: *Everton*
Country: *Brazil*
DOB: *10/05/1997*

If it wasn't for his inconsistent performances, Richarlison could be a lot higher on this list! The Brazilian baller can look like an absolute world-beater when he's flying, but it's often hit or miss as to whether he's in the mood to impress! If he manages to find a way of being more consistent, there's still lots of time for him to unlock his world-class potential!

CONFIDENCE	DRIBBLING	TRICKS	AGILITY	WEAK FOOT
77	88	85	82	75

44 ADAMA TRAORE

Club: *Wolves*
Country: *Spain*
DOB: *25/01/1996*

Even though he's famous for his blistering pace, the Spaniard has shown that he has more to his game! He once clocked 23.48mph against Chelsea in the Prem, and it only takes one or two skill moves to beat a defender when you're running at that speed. He's even started lathering his arms in baby oil so they can't drag him down!

CONFIDENCE	DRIBBLING	TRICKS	AGILITY	WEAK FOOT
80	92	83	85	70

43 PEDRO NETO

Club: *Wolves*
Country: *Portugal*
DOB: *09/03/2000*

As if having to play against Traore wasn't enough, Wolves also have another baller on the opposite flank in the form of Neto! He loves receiving the ball out wide and using his speed to run at opponents! If you can't remember his stunning solo goal v Southampton from 2020-21, we recommend you watch it again!

CONFIDENCE	DRIBBLING	TRICKS	AGILITY	WEAK FOOT
82	79	75	86	75

42 TANGUY NDOMBELE

Club: *Tottenham*
Country: *France*
DOB: *28/12/1996*

We reckon the Frenchman deserves to retain his place in this list purely based on his outrageous goal v Sheffield United in 2020-21! He hooked a brilliant, improvised lob over the goalkeeper to fire his side to an important three points – and it's that ability to produce moments of magic that makes him an absolute baller. Hero!

CONFIDENCE	DRIBBLING	TRICKS	AGILITY	WEAK FOOT
82	84	88	80	80

41 NANI

Club: *Orlando City*
Country: *Portugal*
DOB: *17/11/1986*

It's been a little while since the ex-Man. United hero has featured in this list, but we simply couldn't ignore his brilliant performances for Orlando City in Major League Soccer! The Portuguese winger hasn't lost his appetite for showboating as he's got older – as shown by his ridiculously cheeky backheel goal against Sporting Kansas City in 2021! Tekkers alert!

CONFIDENCE	DRIBBLING	TRICKS	AGILITY	WEAK FOOT
85	86	86	85	85

40
ANTHONY MARTIAL

TOP SKILL!
THE DRAG TO DRAG!

Club: *Man. United*
Country: *France*
DOB: *05/12/1995*

It's fair to say that the Frenchman thrives massively on confidence but, when he's on his game, there aren't many players that can cope with his quick feet! Unfortunately for Martial, he wasn't at his best for Man. United in 2020-21 and missed out on the Euros through injury. Fingers crossed he'll be back to his best in 2021-22!

CONFIDENCE
80

DRIBBLING
90

TRICKS
92

AGILITY
88

WEAK FOOT
85

STARTING OUT!

JACK SAYS: "I got a bad injury when I was 14 years old and, after eight months out, I fell out of love with 11-a-side. My mum said I had to get back into football and told me about a club that played at our local town hall – and it was street football! I trained every day for the first three years, went to uni, and then I've been training every day for the last two years too!"

JACK DOWNER...
PANNA KING!

MATCH catches up with nutmeg extraordinaire JACK DOWNER on his epic journey to becoming an uber baller!

HOW MUCH PRACTICE?

JACK SAYS: "I aim for at least 20 minutes every day. It doesn't sound like very much, but the whole point is that I never want to go backwards. If you leave it four days, the first time you touch the ball you feel a bit rusty. But wherever I have the chance, I'll spend longer – realistically, it ends up being about an hour a day. Over lockdown, I spent about four hours a day training!"

TOP TEKKERS!

JACK SAYS: "The thing about creating tricks is that you're convinced you've created something, but then someone else has actually just done it as well! There's some tricks that I'm 99% sure that I created and I'm the first person to put on the internet! My favourite trick is an old-school one called the Ankle Breaker – it's also my logo! You're standing right on the top of the ball on your tip-toes!"

FOOTY INSPIRATION!

JACK SAYS: "I remember going on YouTube as a child and coming across the iconic video of Ronaldinho's crossbar challenge, then his Joga Bonito video as a kid - and I got obsessed with Ronaldinho! I always looked up to Gareth Bale as well because he moved from wing-back to winger, and that was the transition I wanted to do when I was a right-back playing 11-a-side!"

WORLD CHAMPS!

JACK SAYS: "It's amazing to play in them - it's the moment you're really trying to put all your skills out. There's a crowd, big pressure, you're in an arena you probably haven't played in before and against top players - it's a big adrenaline rush!"

SKILLS OR GOALS?

JACK SAYS: "Skills are as important as you want them to be! For me, half of it is about entertaining - you don't want to just kick the ball into the net. Goals are obviously important - you want to be winning so the other player has to take the ball off you. I've kept the ball for two minutes and 50 seconds in a three-minute game before! When your opponents start getting desperate and want to tackle - that's when the nutmegs will come!"

WHY PANNA RULES!

JACK SAYS: "It's a fun, super-fast, three-minute game that's easy to understand - kick the ball through your opponent's legs or score the most goals and you win! It's not like in a 90-minute match when you get the ball for five minutes - in Panna, you own the ball. It's got the vibe of being a school ground game - that's where I want everyone to be playing it!"

TOP ADVICE!

JACK SAYS: "Train a little bit every day, but also listen to your body - if you're feeling achy or tired, take a little rest! When you really enjoy something you find time to train, so you need to make sure you keep enjoying Panna - nutmeg people, get nutmegged, learn, watch matches, go to tournaments, message your favourite players for advice - and over time, you'll easily be as good as me!"

FIFA SKILLS

BASICS
Here's how to get to grips with the basic FIFA skill moves...

FIFA SKILL MOVES GUIDE

Any arrows that are facing upwards mean you should flick or hold the analogue stick in the direction your player is facing. Simple!

You can find out what your player's skill rating is by checking player information. The more stars they have, the more skilful they are!

You don't have to worry about learning every single trick all at once – in fact, mastering one or two is more effective on FIFA!

BALL ROLL ★★

You can either use this move to open up shooting chances or spot a killer pass for a team-mate, or to get out of the way of a defender's slide tackle and make them look silly!

HOLD: R Stick Left   **OR HOLD:** R Stick Right

R ←   R →

1

2

PERFECT PLAYER
ROBERTO FIRMINO

STEPOVER ★★

You can bust out a few stepovers if you're looking to trick a defender into thinking that you're going to move in a certain direction, before burning off the other way!

ROLL: R Stick Left/Right

R ←   R →

PERFECT PLAYER
CRISTIANO RONALDO

1

2

DRAG BACK ★★

This is a really good move if you need to take a step back and pass it to another player - especially if you're being pressed really hard by the opposition. Tekkers!

HOLD: R1/RB + L1/LB then L Stick Down

PERFECT PLAYER
TONI KROOS

BODY FEINT ★★

There aren't many moves that are more effective on FIFA than the body feint. It's mainly used to beat defenders, as well as to create space for one of your team-mates!

FLICK: R Stick Left/Right

PERFECT PLAYER
EDEN HAZARD

39

NICOLAS PEPE

Club: Arsenal
Country: Ivory Coast
DOB: 29/05/1995

It took him a while to get going, but the Ivory Coast winger is starting to show his doubters why Arsenal splashed out a record £72 million on him! He's been nicknamed 'The Ivorian Arjen Robben' by The Gunners, but it's fair to say he's still got some way to go before he can be seriously compared to the ex-Bayern Munich superstar!

CONFIDENCE 80

DRIBBLING 93

TRICKS 90

AGILITY 92

WEAK FOOT 75

38

SAID BENRAHMA

Club: *West Ham*
Country: *Algeria*
DOB: *10/08/1995*

It's not difficult to see why West Ham were so keen on signing the Algerian from Brentford! He's built up an amazing highlights reel of showboating since moving to England, but he backs up all his wicked tricks with end product! One of his former coaches once said that the winger could nutmeg a mermaid. LOL!

CONFIDENCE	DRIBBLING	TRICKS	AGILITY	WEAK FOOT
80	80	90	84	80

37

PHIL FODEN

Club: *Man. City*
Country: *England*
DOB: *28/05/2000*

He's nicknamed the 'Stockport Iniesta' because he pulls tons of tricks out of the bag! Up until a few years ago, he was still humiliating his mates on the streets of his hometown! Pep Guardiola has described him as the most talented player he's ever worked with, which is some compliment given that he's worked with Lionel Messi at Barcelona!

CONFIDENCE	DRIBBLING	TRICKS	AGILITY	WEAK FOOT
85	78	83	87	75

36

MARCELO

Club: *Real Madrid*
Country: *Brazil*
DOB: *12/05/1988*

Marcelo might be approaching the end of his career, but he's still entertaining us with his brilliant skill, pacy attacking and all-round excellence at Real Madrid! The Brazilian is arguably one of the most skilful defenders of all-time and nobody is safe when coming up against him in a one-v-one situation – even his own team-mates in training have been left red-faced!

TOP SKILL!
EPIC FIRST TOUCH!

CONFIDENCE	DRIBBLING	TRICKS	AGILITY	WEAK FOOT
87	88	88	85	86

35
GABRIEL JESUS

Club: Man. City
Country: Brazil
DOB: 03/04/1997

Having grown up on the streets of Sao Paulo, it's no surprise that the Brazilian is one of the most skilful strikers in the Premier League! Every Brazilian is expected to bust out a few stepovers and roulettes every so often, but he's got the footballing intelligence to know when it's appropriate!

CONFIDENCE	DRIBBLING	TRICKS	AGILITY	WEAK FOOT
85	86	86	91	75

34
RAPHINHA

Club: Leeds
Country: Brazil
DOB: 14/12/1996

From one brilliant Brazilian to another... Raphinha's been an awesome addition to Marcelo Bielsa's exciting team at Leeds! It's not a style of play that normally suits tricky players, but the youngster has the work rate to go with his attacking flair. We can't wait to see even more of him in 2021-22!

CONFIDENCE	DRIBBLING	TRICKS	AGILITY	WEAK FOOT
87	84	80	86	75

33
MOHAMED SALAH

TOP SKILL!
THE BODY FEINT!

Club: Liverpool
Country: Egypt
DOB: 15/06/1992

He's nicknamed the 'Egyptian Messi' because his biggest strength is his amazing dribbling skills! As well as having blistering pace on the ball, he's got one of the most powerful left-footed strikes in the Premier League, which is why he continues to bag tons of goals and assists for Liverpool!

CONFIDENCE	DRIBBLING	TRICKS	AGILITY	WEAK FOOT
94	92	87	91	75

DIMITRI PAYET

32

Club: Marseille
Country: France
DOB: 29/03/1987

Although the Frenchman has tons of epic skills up his sleeve, he's most well-known for being a set-piece specialist! He's scored countless bending free-kicks that defy physics throughout his career, and he's still strutting his stuff in Ligue 1 with Marseille! We just wish we got to enjoy watching him for a bit longer in the Premier League!

CONFIDENCE	DRIBBLING	TRICKS	AGILITY	WEAK FOOT
83	90	86	78	89

31

ANSU FATI

Club: Barcelona
Country: Spain
DOB: 31/10/2002

Even though he barely played any football due to injury in 2020-21, the Spaniard is still deserving of a place in this list! He's the brightest prospect to emerge from Barcelona's famous La Masia academy for several years and has the natural ability to develop into one of the world's best skillers!

CONFIDENCE	DRIBBLING	TRICKS	AGILITY	WEAK FOOT
85	79	77	89	80

30

ISCO

Club: Real Madrid
Country: Spain
DOB: 21/04/1992

He's not played as much football as he would've liked over the last few years at Real Madrid, but there still aren't many players who have quicker feet than the silky Spain playmaker! He's just as capable of picking out an inch-perfect pass as he is dribbling effortlessly through two or three challenges. Legend!

CONFIDENCE	DRIBBLING	TRICKS	AGILITY	WEAK FOOT
80	92	88	86	93

WORDFIT

Fit the skillers that just missed out on this year's countdown into this massive grid!

Ben Arfa	Fernandes	Ozil
Bernard	Hernani	Piatti
Bernardeschi	Ibrahimovic	Promes
Bolasie	Januzaj	Quaresma
Boufal	Maddison	Ribery
Cherki	Mane	Saka
Deulofeu	Marlos	Sarr
Draxler	Martins	Shaqiri
Dybala	McGeady	Tadic
El Shaarawy	Odegaard	Willian

IBRAHIMOVIC

5 QUESTIONS ON...

ALLAN SAINT-MAXIMIN

1 Is the tricky winger younger or older than his Newcastle team-mate Miguel Almiron?

2 True or False? Allan has made over 100 appearances for his national side France!

3 Name the class French side ASM played for before joining Newcastle back in 2019!

4 Who did he score his first Newcastle goal against - Sheffield United, Burnley or Aston Villa?

5 True or False? The winger spent £180 on a Gucci headband to wear during matches!

SPOT THE BALL!

Mark where you think the ball should be in this cool action shot!

ANSWERS ON P60

FIFA SKILLS

HEELYS
Use these class heel-based moves to tear past your opponent!

HEEL FLICK ★★★

You can use this awesome move to quickly skip past defenders, but make sure they're not already too close to you as they'll be able to easily intercept the ball!

FLICK: R Stick Up   **THEN FLICK:** R Stick Down

R ↑   R ↓

1

2

PERFECT PLAYER
KYLIAN MBAPPE

HEEL CHOP ★★★

There's no better way of quickly changing direction than using this elite move, and certain players like Cristiano Ronaldo are brilliant at it - on FIFA and in real life!

HOLD: L2/LT + Fake Shot

L2 / LT + ○ / B + X / A

1

PERFECT PLAYER
CRISTIANO RONALDO

2

HEEL FLICK TURN ★★★★★

HOLD: R1/RB + Right Stick   **FLICK:** R Stick Up + Down

If you're looking for a slightly trickier heel-based move to try out, then this is a great way of embarrassing a defender before properly bursting past them!

PERFECT PLAYER

JADON SANCHO

DRAG TO DRAG ★★★★

HOLD: L2/LT + Fake Shot + Release L Stick

You can use this move to set up a shooting opportunity. Be aware that this is a four-star skill move though, so can only be performed by a certain number of players!

PERFECT PLAYER

MEMPHIS DEPAY

29

JOAO FELIX

Club: *Atletico Madrid*
Country: *Portugal*
DOB: *10/11/1999*

It's fair to say that the 2019 Golden Boy winner hasn't quite lived up to expectations since joining Atletico for £113 million from Benfica! That being said, he's still more than capable of producing a moment of magic! His backheel passes and first-touch skills have already seen him compared with Portugal team-mate Cristiano Ronaldo!

CONFIDENCE	DRIBBLING	TRICKS	AGILITY	WEAK FOOT
85	84	86	86	85

28

EDEN HAZARD

Club: *Real Madrid*
Country: *Belgium*
DOB: *07/01/1991*

Hazard left the Premier League over three years ago as the best dribbler and top assister, but he's had an absolute nightmare since! He finished in ninth place on this list last year, but we had no choice but to move him way down after another injury-plagued season in Spain!

CONFIDENCE	DRIBBLING	TRICKS	AGILITY	WEAK FOOT
84	90	88	92	90

27

EDUARDO CAMAVINGA

Club: *Real Madrid*
Country: *France*
DOB: *10/11/2002*

The box-to-box midfielder became the youngest player to represent and score for France in over 100 years in 2020! He opened his account for his country in style by scoring a spectacular overhead-kick against Ukraine! With his quick feet and insane dribbling skills, we can see him being even higher up this list next year! His potential is massive!

TOP SKILL! THE SHIMMY!

CONFIDENCE	DRIBBLING	TRICKS	AGILITY	WEAK FOOT
84	77	78	77	75

26

LEROY SANE

Club: *Bayern Munich*
Country: *Germany*
DOB: *11/01/1996*

In MATCH's opinion, Sane's position on this list depends on his confidence levels! He's one of those players who can really struggle when he doesn't feel comfortable, or look like an absolute world-beater when he's flying – and then deserve to be ten spots higher instead!

TOP SKILL!
THE BODY FEINT!

CONFIDENCE	DRIBBLING	TRICKS	AGILITY	WEAK FOOT
80	96	85	93	77

25

THIAGO

Club: *Liverpool*
Country: *Spain*
DOB: *11/04/1991*

Thiago's been described by many as the man to make the pass before the assist, which is why his numbers aren't always the most impressive! He's got the creativity, vision and intelligence to pick defences apart, which is why we're backing him to get back to his best over the next few months at Liverpool!

CONFIDENCE	DRIBBLING	TRICKS	AGILITY	WEAK FOOT
86	90	90	91	84

24

PHILIPPE COUTINHO

Club: *Barcelona*
Country: *Brazil*
DOB: *12/06/1992*

Coutinho was born and raised in Rio de Janeiro, the same city as Brazilian icon Ronaldo, so it's no surprise that he's got tons of tricks up his sleeve! He's well-known for nutmegging defenders, but it's his curving long-range shots that make him a constant threat around the edge of the area!

CONFIDENCE	DRIBBLING	TRICKS	AGILITY	WEAK FOOT
84	90	88	92	90

23
NABIL FEKIR

Club: *Real Betis*
Country: *France*
DOB: *18/07/1993*

We expected bigger things from the Frenchman after he won Ligue 1 Young Player of the Year in 2014-15! He hasn't reached the heights that many thought he would, but he still has an uncanny ability to manoeuvre himself out of tight spaces! He knows that when the ball comes his way, he can make something happen at once!

CONFIDENCE	DRIBBLING	TRICKS	AGILITY	WEAK FOOT
84	90	88	92	90

22
KINGSLEY COMAN

Club: *Bayern Munich*
Country: *France*
DOB: *13/06/1996*

Since his title-clinching goal in the 2019-20 Champions League final, the wing wizard has been enjoying the best period of his career! The Frenchman's pace and trickery on the ball, as well as his wicked dribbling ability, make him an absolute nightmare for defenders to deal with!

CONFIDENCE	DRIBBLING	TRICKS	AGILITY	WEAK FOOT
85	92	95	92	90

21
MEMPHIS DEPAY

Club: *Barcelona*
Country: *Netherlands*
DOB: *13/02/1994*

Despite a bad spell in England with Man. United, Depay has since proven that he's a world-class baller! The Dutchman's pace, eye-catching skills and ice-cold finishing saw Spanish giants Barcelona snap him up last summer! He's often leaving defenders embarrassed with his soul-destroying skill!

CONFIDENCE	DRIBBLING	TRICKS	AGILITY	WEAK FOOT
90	84	94	85	80

★ TOP SKILL!
THE CLASSIC STEPOVER!

20

JUAN CUADRADO

TOP SKILL!
THE HEEL FLICK PASS!

JUVENTUS

Club: *Juventus*
Country: *Colombia*
DOB: *26/05/1988*

Zlatan Ibrahimovic and Luis Suarez aren't the only players who seem to be getting better with age – just ask Juan! The veteran winger is proof if it were ever needed that not all players in the latter stages of their career are slow and doddery! He's absolutely smashing it in Italy and loves dancing past opponents!

CONFIDENCE
90

DRIBBLING
90

TRICKS
90

AGILITY
91

WEAK FOOT
78

AGUSKA

MATCH catches up with AGUSKA MNICH, a two-time world champion, to chat about her epic freestyling career!

BEING A FREESTYLER!

AGUSKA SAYS: "I started doing freestyle for myself, I never really thought I'd be competing! I just did it because I loved it! Freestyle is beautiful because you are creating your own style. There are a lot of things you need to learn every single day. It's not just standing there and doing one trick. It's about creating new things all the time!"

TRAINING HARD!

AGUSKA SAYS: "Practising every single day, even if it's hard and even if you don't feel like you can do it, is the most important thing. If you believe in something, you can do it! At the start it was difficult as there were a lot of distractions and a lot of people who told me that I couldn't do it. Even if I felt like I didn't want to train, I still went!"

HER JOURNEY!

AGUSKA SAYS: "I was playing football and then one day I saw two guys doing freestyle and I just fell in love! I was like, 'Guys, what is this?' and then they just explained that you don't kick the ball, you just do tricks! The day after I started from scratch – I didn't even know how to do one kick-up! I wanted to do an 'Around the World' and it took me two weeks to learn that trick, and after that I wanted more!"

MNICH

...FREESTYLE STAR!

FAVOURITE MOMENT!

AGUSKA SAYS: "The 2018 Red Bull Street Style in Poland! I won my first championship which was the most important for me! I finished fourth in 2014 and second in 2016, so I just wanted to get the next one! Once I won, I can't even describe the feeling!"

FAVOURITE TRICKS!

AGUSKA SAYS: "I would say handstands as you have a lot of variation! I'd say they are my favourite right now. I'm still learning and always looking to improve. That's why they are making me really happy as I'm seeing progress. I love to do anything in freestyle, though!"

TOP ADVICE!

AGUSKA SAYS: "If you want to start freestyle, just take a football and go outside! Just know what trick you want to learn and keep going! Right now, it's amazing because you can learn freestyle from the internet. You can just search for tutorials of the certain tricks you want to learn, and that's how you can get into it. It's much easier than it was ten years ago when they weren't there!"

SOCIAL MEDIA!

AGUSKA SAYS: "I've been into social media for about three years and it's big! It's an amazing way of promoting freestyle, inspiring people and teaching people as well! It's a way for everybody to find out what freestyle is all about. We are living in the best time right now as you have connections with everyone!"

CROSSWORD

Use the clues to fill in MATCH's tricky crossword puzzle!

ACROSS

2. Number of league titles that Cristiano Ronaldo won at Real Madrid! (3)

5. Number of league titles Thiago won at Barcelona! (4)

6. Sick boot brand that Angel Di Maria wears! (6)

8. Country that Phil Foden scored his first England goals against! (7)

9. French team that Real Betis signed Nabil Fekir from back in 2019! (4)

11. Shirt number that Paul Pogba wears for France! (3)

12. Position that Leicester baller Christian Fuchs normally plays! (4,4)

14. Foot that Leroy Sane prefers to use! (4)

16. Huge Italian team that signed Philippe Coutinho as a 16-year-old way back in 2008! (5,5)

18. Cristiano Ronaldo's mega weird 'O Robo' nickname in English! (3,5)

DOWN

1. African country that speedy winger Samuel Chukwueze represents! (7)

3. Month that Spain young gun Ansu Fati was born! (7)

4. South American country where Neymar was born! (6)

6. Prem team where Martin Odegaard spent the second half of 2020-21 on loan! (7)

7. Number of league goals that Raphinha scored for Leeds in 2020-21! (3)

10. Boot brand that Man. City's Riyad Mahrez wears! (4)

13. Number of countries that Kingsley Coman has played professional footy in! (5)

14. English city that Crystal Palace wonderkid Eberechi Eze grew up in! (6)

15. Shirt number that Marcus Rashford wears for Man. United! (3)

17. French team that tricky wingers Allan Saint-Maximin and Hatem Ben Arfa have both played for! (4)

THE NICKNAME GAME

Have a go at matching the world-class trick machines to their awesome nicknames!

Douglas Costa	Neymar	Hakim Ziyech	Lionel Messi	Angel Di Maria	Martin Odegaard
1	2	3	4	5	6

A	B	C	D	E	F
The King	Flash	Noodle	The Flea	The Gem	The Wizard

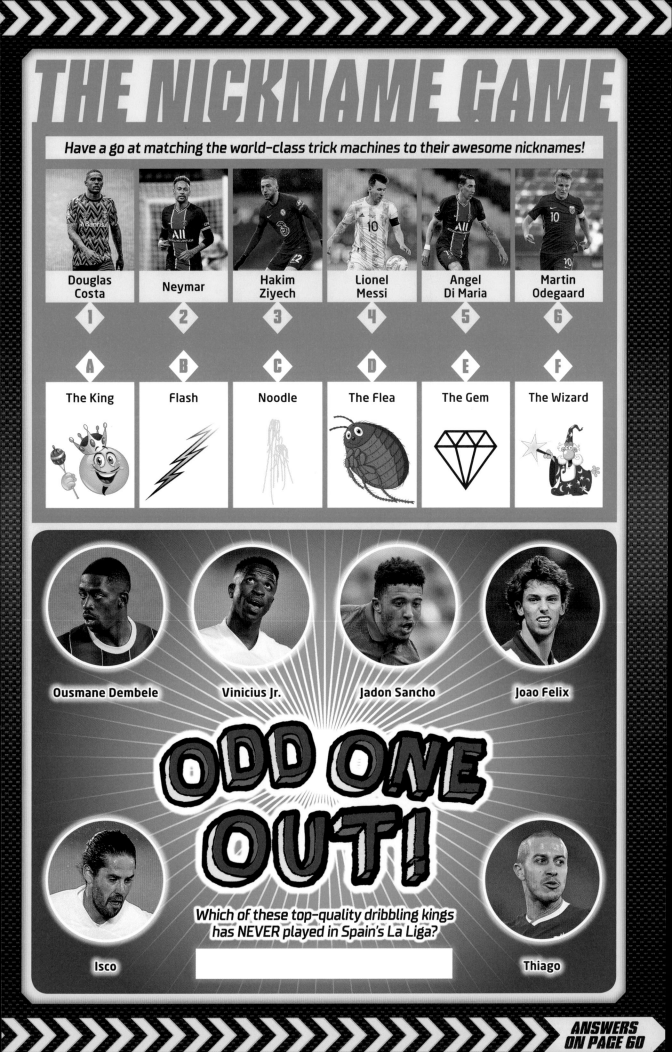

Ousmane Dembele

Vinicius Jr.

Jadon Sancho

Joao Felix

ODD ONE OUT!

Which of these top-quality dribbling kings has NEVER played in Spain's La Liga?

Isco

Thiago

ANSWERS ON PAGE 60

TOP SKILL!
THE ELASTICO!

19
MARCUS RASHFORD

Club: *Man. United*
Country: *England*
DOB: *31/10/1997*

As a football-mad youngster, Rashford would spend hours watching his Man. United idols Cristiano Ronaldo and Wayne Rooney in action, before practising his new skills around the house! Injuries might have held him back slightly over the past year or so, but he's still one of the most exciting players on the planet – he's the king of the Elastico!

CONFIDENCE
88

DRIBBLING
86

TRICKS
94

AGILITY
89

WEAK FOOT
78

18

ROBERTO FIRMINO

Club: *Liverpool*
Country: *Brazil*
DOB: *02/10/1991*

The Brazilian might not score as many goals as he'd like to, but Jurgen Klopp is always quick to highlight that he offers so much more to Liverpool! Even when he's not finding the back of the net, Firmino is always capable of producing a moment of skill to embarrass defenders. When he does score, his no-look finishes prove that he's one of the cheekiest players in world football right now!

TOP SKILL!
THE NO-LOOK GOAL!

CONFIDENCE	DRIBBLING	TRICKS	AGILITY	WEAK FOOT
90	88	93	81	88

17

PAUL POGBA

Club: *Man. United*
Country: *France*
DOB: *15/03/1993*

There aren't many better sights than watching the France World Cup-winning midfielder playing at his best! Not many players in world football have as much natural ability as Pogba. He makes pulling off a roulette look so, so easy! He could move even further up this list next year!

CONFIDENCE	DRIBBLING	TRICKS	AGILITY	WEAK FOOT
88	84	92	80	93

16

OUSMANE DEMBELE

Club: *Barcelona*
Country: *France*
DOB: *15/05/1997*

The forward managed to stay injury-free at Barca in 2020-21 – the first time he's done that since arriving at the Nou Camp to replace Neymar – meaning it was the first proper chance we got to see his true potential! He's got some work to do on his finishing, but his top tekkers still scare defenders!

CONFIDENCE	DRIBBLING	TRICKS	AGILITY	WEAK FOOT
88	84	92	80	93

15

SAMUEL CHUKWUEZE

Club: *Villarreal*
Country: *Nigeria*
DOB: *22/05/1999*

Chukwueze has moved up two places from last year's countdown! The left-footed winger has the speed, quality and technique to become a world-class player if he continues to perform at this level! He helped Villarreal win the Europa League in 2020-21, and he'll be hoping it's the first of many trophies he wins over the course of his career!

TOP SKILL!
THE FAKE PASS EXIT!

CONFIDENCE	DRIBBLING	TRICKS	AGILITY	WEAK FOOT
89	85	91	91	76

14

MARTIN ODEGAARD

Club: *Arsenal*
Country: *Norway*
DOB: *17/12/1998*

The Norway captain's epic loan spell at Arsenal worked wonders for his confidence! As well as getting regular footy, Odegaard was also one of their standout performers, so it was no surprise when The Gunners splashed out £30 million to sign him from Real Madrid! He's mega creative and has massive potential!

CONFIDENCE	DRIBBLING	TRICKS	AGILITY	WEAK FOOT
93	90	94	85	70

13

RODRYGO

Club: *Real Madrid*
Country: *Brazil*
DOB: *09/01/2001*

Real Madrid have tons of talented young players, but nobody has as much potential as Rodrygo! The Brazilian is nicknamed the 'Next Neymar' in his home country – and he's beginning to live up to those comparisons! We've seen on countless occasions in La Liga how he's able to leave defenders in the dust with his skills and athleticism!

CONFIDENCE	DRIBBLING	TRICKS	AGILITY	WEAK FOOT
95	93	93	86	78

---

34 MATCH!

12
DOUGLAS COSTA

Club: *Gremio*
Country: *Brazil*
DOB: *14/09/1990*

Juventus announced last May that the Brazilian would be heading back to his homeland to join Gremio on a season-long loan for 2021-22! It wasn't so long ago that he was one of the best playmakers in Italy, so he's still got more than enough in his locker to be a big hit at Gremio!

CONFIDENCE	DRIBBLING	TRICKS	AGILITY	WEAK FOOT
89	92	95	93	79

11
LIONEL MESSI

Club: *PSG*
Country: *Argentina*
DOB: *24/06/1987*

We reckon the six-time Ballon d'Or winner can carry on playing at the highest level for a few more years yet! Season after season, Leo proves why he's the world's best dribbler – and his confidence will be as high as ever after moving to PSG and winning the Copa America last summer!

CONFIDENCE	DRIBBLING	TRICKS	AGILITY	WEAK FOOT
99	95	85	93	85

10
ALLAN SAINT-MAXIMIN

Club: *Newcastle*
Country: *France*
DOB: *12/03/1997*

The Frenchman's combination of electric pace, deadly dribbling and sick skill has made him a firm fans' favourite at St. James' Park! The Magpies could have been relegated from the Premier League in 2020-21 if it wasn't for Saint-Maximin's ability to win a game on his own! We'd recommend following him on social media as he's a funny guy off the pitch as well!

TOP SKILL!
THE STEPOVER!

CONFIDENCE	DRIBBLING	TRICKS	AGILITY	WEAK FOOT
93	90	95	93	87

FIFA SKILLS

JUGGLING
These jaw-dropping moves will really impress your mates!

LACES FLICK UP ★★★★★

This move is a really simple way for you to get the ball up into the air! Once you've got the hang of this, there are tons of different skill moves you can add to it!

PRESS: L2/LT + Hold R1/RB

1

2

PERFECT PLAYER
HARRY KANE

FLICK UP FOR VOLLEY ★★★★★

If you're looking to smash a mind-blowing volley into the top corner with the player you're currently in control of, then just flick the ball up for yourself!

HOLD: Left Stick Up

PERFECT PLAYER
RAHEEM STERLING

1

2

AROUND THE WORLD ★★★★★

If you manage to pull this incredible move off, then your opponent will be left so mesmerised that they won't stand a chance of tackling you straight afterwards!

TURN: Right Stick 360° Clockwise

OR

360° Anti-Clockwise

R → ↓ ← ↑   R ← ↓ → ↑

PERFECT PLAYER
NEYMAR

T. AROUND THE WORLD ★★★★★

If you're looking for a slightly different variation of the Around The World to mix things up a bit, then this version of the trick is just as effective – and even more cool!

TURN: Right Stick 360 Degrees then Flick Right Stick Up

R → ↓ ← ↑ + R ↑

PERFECT PLAYER
WILFRIED ZAHA

ULTIMATE SKILLER!

1

Five-time world champion football freestyler Andrew Henderson creates the world's ultimate skiller using ballers past and present!

MENTALITY
Cristiano Ronaldo

1

ANDREW SAYS: "Cristiano Ronaldo! Even though he's so good and has achieved so much in the game, it's really good to see that he's still in the mindset of wanting to learn and always get better. He never gets too cocky thinking he's the best. He's a good person to be at the top of football!"

4

BRAIN
Zinedine Zidane

2

ANDREW SAYS: "He's not playing anymore, but he's still present as a manager - Zinedine Zidane! The way he used to think on the ball, he was so clever. He's taken his knowledge into coaching! Another former player that comes to mind is Andrea Pirlo!"

5

6

VISION
Neymar

3

ANDREW SAYS: "Back in the day, I would've said David Beckham, but let's go for Neymar! Although he's a crazy skiller, he sees ways to move through players - in and out of players - very well! He's really crafty in that way. It's all his time playing football on the street as a kid, which gives him that small touch and close control to react and see things!"

7

2

3

SWAGGER
Paul Pogba

4

ANDREW SAYS: "I've got to go for France midfielder Paul Pogba – he's the first player that comes to mind! He's just so confident – he dances around and has that confidence!"

AGILITY
Kylian Mbappe

5

ANDREW SAYS: "Kylian Mbappe! The guy's absolutely rapid! It was during the 2018 World Cup when I noticed it the most – his first two or three touches, he was able to gain ten yards on his opponent. He can really switch it on quick. Insane acceleration and agility!"

6

BALL CONTROL
Marcelo

ANDREW SAYS: "Marcelo! If you look online, there are some balls that just get flown from the other side of the pitch and he just touches them down and looks the other way – totally chilled out, like he doesn't even care, but that is hours and hours of practice! That's the Brazilian spirit – they're crazy those guys!"

QUICK FEET
Cristiano Ronaldo

7

ANDREW SAYS: "Nowadays he's not seen as much as a player with quick feet, but Ronaldo's incredible. I've seen it live – the way he moves his feet, he's so good at it. He's changed his game now that he's a bit older, but when he first played for Man. United, his stepovers and the movement were inspiring for me!"

8

TEKKERS
Christian Fuchs

8

ANDREW SAYS: "I've always used Neymar, so I'm not going to say him again! You would not believe it, but Christian Fuchs is incredible at freestyle. He can do something like 20 Around The Worlds in a row and a double Around The World. For a defender, you'd never imagine it, but he's really good!"

Andrew Henderson was speaking at the launch of his new book, How To Be A Better Footballer.

9
HAKIM ZIYECH

TOP SKILL!
THE BODY FEINT!

Club: *Chelsea*

Country: *Morocco*

DOB: *19/03/1993*

One of Ziyech's most effective skill moves is literally just cutting inside from the right flank, and then looking to cross or attempt a through-ball to one of his team-mates. He has some top tekkers too, though – it was his jaw-dropping drag back against Sheffield United in the 2020-21 season that really had MATCH drooling. He left the defender totally rooted to the turf!

CONFIDENCE
95

DRIBBLING
92

TRICKS
93

AGILITY
92

WEAK FOOT
80

8

ANGEL DI MARIA

Club: PSG
Country: Argentina
DOB: 14/02/1988

We reckon the ex-Man. United flop might be one of the most underrated ballers on the planet, mainly because he's overshadowed by Kylian Mbappe and Neymar at PSG! Di Maria has been a reliable lock-picker throughout his career, and always has the ability to create big chances with his spellbinding feet and brilliant footballing brain! The Rabona is one of his signature moves!

CONFIDENCE	DRIBBLING	TRICKS	AGILITY	WEAK FOOT
89	87	92	86	88

7

CRISTIANO RONALDO

Club: Man. United
Country: Portugal
DOB: 05/02/1985

It's fair to say that he's adapted his style of play as he's got older, but we'd be lying if we said we didn't love it when Cristiano turns back the clock and decides to turn on the skills! He's still more than capable of producing a throwback to his days as a wicked wonderkid with a series of stepovers, leaving defenders completely baffled in the process! He'll go down as one of the most legendary skillers of all time!

CONFIDENCE	DRIBBLING	TRICKS	AGILITY	WEAK FOOT
98	89	95	87	94

6

VINICIUS JUNIOR

TOP SKILL!
THE OUTSIDE SCOOP!

Club: *Real Madrid*
Country: *Brazil*
DOB: *12/07/2000*

Just as he was this time last year, Vinicius is still receiving a lot of stick from some fans over his finishing, and new Real Madrid boss Carlo Ancelotti says it's something that he wants to see the Brazilian improve on! The jet-heeled winger is still in the early stages of his career though, and he has already produced some jaw-dropping pieces of skill in big games. He just needs to work on his end product!

CONFIDENCE	DRIBBLING	TRICKS	AGILITY	WEAK FOOT
96	95	96	97	85

5

KYLIAN MBAPPE

TOP SKILL!
THE FAKE RABONA!

Club: *PSG*
Country: *France*
DOB: *20/12/1998*

One youngster who certainly doesn't need to work on his finishing is World Cup winner Mbappe! Even though PSG didn't win Ligue 1 in 2020-21, the Frenchman still netted 27 goals in 31 matches to make it his most prolific season yet! He's not all about goals though, as he proved against Monaco when he picked the ball up inside his own box before dribbling the length of the pitch in an incredible display of skill!

CONFIDENCE	DRIBBLING	TRICKS	AGILITY	WEAK FOOT
98	95	93	95	88

4

WILFRIED ZAHA

TOP SKILL!
THE HOCUS POCUS!

DID YOU KNOW?
ZAHA SCORED 11 GOALS IN 29 APPEARANCES IN ALL COMPETITIONS IN 2020-21 - THE MOST HE'S SCORED IN A SINGLE SEASON IN HIS CAREER!

Club: Crystal Palace
Country: Ivory Coast
DOB: 10/11/1992

Even if you forced Zaha to play with a tennis ball, he'd still be able to dribble his way past defenders with ease - in fact, that's exactly how his journey to becoming one of the world's biggest ballers began! As a youngster, he used to practise his dribbling skills in the living room with his sister after being inspired by Ronaldinho!

CONFIDENCE
97

DRIBBLING
96

TRICKS
98

AGILITY
94

WEAK FOOT
84

BRAIN-BUSTER!

How well do you know some of footy's best tricksters?

1. True or False? Crystal Palace signed Eberechi Eze from the same club that they signed Wilfried Zaha!

2. Which Brazilian team did legend Ronaldinho not play for – Flamengo, Fluminense, Gremio or Sao Paulo?

3. Which English side did Man. City sign silky Algeria baller Riyad Mahrez from in 2018?

4. How many Serie A games did Paul Pogba play for Juventus – more or less than 100?

5. Which Portuguese side did Joao Felix start his senior career with - Benfica, Porto or Braga?

6. Which African country does Arsenal winger Nicolas Pepe play for – Ivory Coast, Ghana or Algeria?

7. How old was Ansu Fati when he made his La Liga debut for Spanish giants Barcelona in 2019?

8. Who was Kylian Mbappe's footy idol when he was growing up – Leo Messi or Cristiano Ronaldo?

9. How much did Liverpool pay Hoffenheim to sign Roberto Firmino – more or less than £30 million?

10. Name the awesome boot brand that England wing wizard Jadon Sancho loves to wear!

1 ....
2 ....
3 ....
4 ....
5 ....
6 ....
7 ....
8 ....
9 ....
10 ....

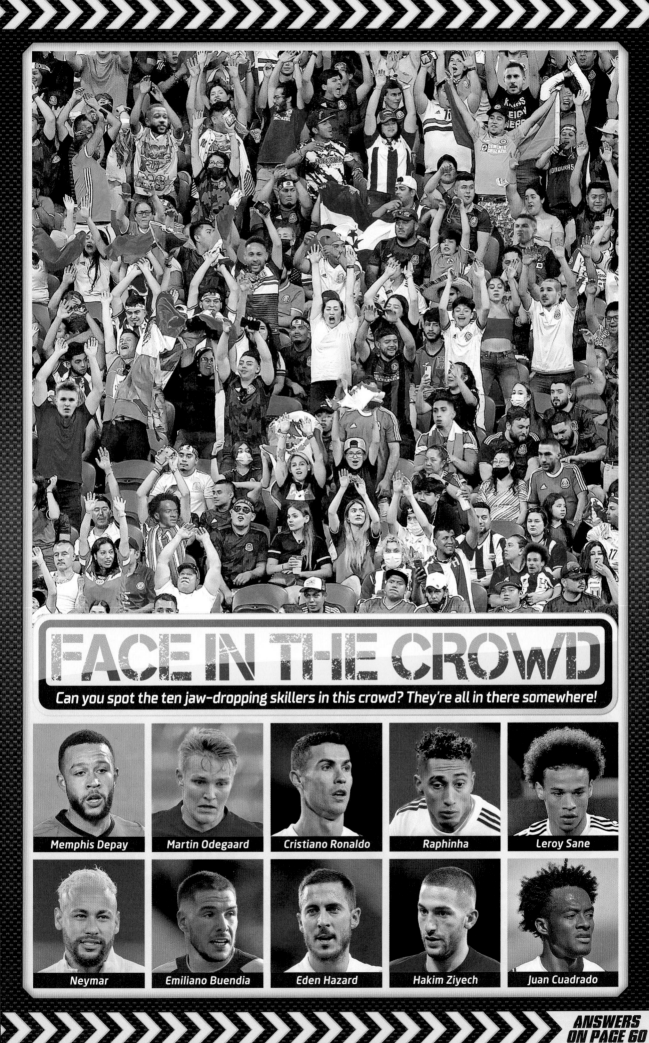

FACE IN THE CROWD

Can you spot the ten jaw-dropping skillers in this crowd? They're all in there somewhere!

Memphis Depay

Martin Odegaard

Cristiano Ronaldo

Raphinha

Leroy Sane

Neymar

Emiliano Buendia

Eden Hazard

Hakim Ziyech

Juan Cuadrado

ANSWERS ON PAGE 60

BEN NUTTALL
...RECORD-BREAKING BALLER!

MATCH catches up with BEN NUTTALL, a world record-breaking freestyler, to chat about his awesome transition from a footballer to a top trickster!

HIS JOURNEY!

BEN SAYS: "I've always been into skills! I've played football since I was young, but I was more interested in the skills. I always thought that was the best thing about the game. I used to watch clips of Ronaldinho and other skilful players like him. It got to the point where I was more interested in doing skills on the side of the pitch than actually playing in the match!"

HERO GROWING UP!

BEN SAYS: "I'd say my hero was definitely Ronaldinho, as well as Diego Maradona. I think kids growing up nowadays look up to players like Neymar!"

TRAINING ALONE!

BEN SAYS: "It's definitely different to being in a team but I like not having a coach telling me what to do and being able to practise whenever I want! I don't have to rely on my team-mates. In freestyle, I can just rely on myself and get out of it what I put in. Sometimes it can get a bit lonely when you're practising on your own, but I think on the whole I've really enjoyed it!"

ACE OPPORTUNITIES!

BEN SAYS: "I'd say my favourite moment was performing during half-time at a game between Arsenal and Man. United at the Emirates Stadium! I've also got to perform in front of Usain Bolt and Mo Farah! I was on their table at a dinner event for Soccer Aid. It's easy to forget that they're world superstars! I always get a bit nervous at events like that, but as soon as I'm doing the skills, the adrenaline takes over!"

STAYING MOTIVATED!

BEN SAYS: "It's always just been fun for me! Sometimes it takes so long to master a particular skill and you'll fail a thousand times before you get it. I think the fun bit is seeing your own progression. I've always been really motivated to keep progressing and keep getting better. It's quite an addictive feeling when you can see yourself getting better!"

SOCIAL MEDIA!

BEN SAYS: "It's weird because I kind of grew up with it. When I first started doing freestyle, Instagram and TikTok weren't a thing. You do have to use it wisely and limit yourself, but there are so many positives! It's a tool that I can use to try to inspire kids and get them involved in freestyle. I also still watch other people's clips myself to try to get motivation from them!"

TOP ADVICE!

BEN SAYS: "Firstly, if you want to get into freestyle, then you've got to enjoy it! It can be frustrating when you're wanting to progress as it takes a lot of practice and dedication. You've just got to keep going and never give up. It's important to remember to maintain that element of it being a bit of fun, though!"

MATCH! 47

3

JADON SANCHO

TOP SKILL!
THE CRUYFF TURN!

DID YOU KNOW?
FORMER ENGLAND U19 TEAM-MATE REISS NELSON WAS ONE OF SANCHO'S BEST FRIENDS WHEN HE WAS YOUNGER!

Club: Man. United
Country: England
DOB: 25/03/2000

CONFIDENCE	96
DRIBBLING	96
TRICKS	96
AGILITY	95
WEAK FOOT	88

Pep Guardiola hasn't got too many things wrong since joining Man. City, but he must have regrets over losing Sancho to Borussia Dortmund in 2017! The winger's been in fantastic form over the last two years and benefitted from a telepathic partnership with Erling Haaland in 2020-21! Now we can't wait to see him tear it up in the Premier League!

2

RIYAD MAHREZ

TOP SKILL!
THE STOP AND GO!

DID YOU KNOW?
IN 2020-21, MAHREZ BECAME THE SIXTH AFRICAN PLAYER TO HIT 100 GOAL INVOLVEMENTS IN THE PREMIER LEAGUE. LEGEND!

Club: *Man. City*
Country: *Algeria*
DOB: *21/02/1991*

Just imagine if Sancho HAD stayed at Man. City - they'd have the trickiest wingers on the planet with Mahrez on the other flank too! The trickster moves up two places from last year's countdown after another jaw-dropping campaign at the Etihad - he was the standout player on their way to the Champions League final!

CONFIDENCE
96

DRIBBLING
95

TRICKS
95

AGILITY
95

WEAK FOOT
91

NEYMAR

Club: *PSG*
Country: *Brazil*
DOB: *05/02/1992*

You guessed it! Neymar has been crowned as MATCH's No.1 for the fourth year in a row – and who can argue? When watching the megastar pull off all his tricks, it's easy to forget that he's competing against some of the best players in the world! It must be a nightmare having to defend against him knowing that you're likely to end up in a highlights reel on YouTube!

TOP SKILL!
THE RAINBOW FLICK!

DID YOU KNOW?

NEYMAR IS THE SECOND ALL-TIME TOP GOALSCORER FOR BRAZIL, AND HE ISN'T TOO FAR OFF BREAKING PELE'S 77-GOAL TALLY!

CONFIDENCE
98

DRIBBLING
97

TRICKS
99

AGILITY
95

WEAK FOOT
90

STAT ATTACK!

NEYMAR

NEYMAR is our gold medal winner once again, so check out some of the sickest stats and facts from his career!

4

He signed a new four-year contract at PSG worth £26 million-a-year in May!

1

Since 2013-14, nobody has picked up as many assists in the Champions League as Neymar!

198

His £198 million move to PSG in 2017 made him the world's most expensive player!

7

Neymar became part of Portuguesa Santista Club in 1999, when he was just seven years old!

20

Neymar is the first player to score 20 goals for two different teams in the history of the Champo League!

95

Neymar's net worth is around $95 million according to Forbes. Wowzers!

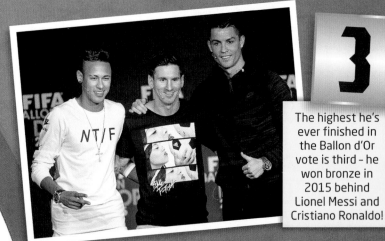

3

The highest he's ever finished in the Ballon d'Or vote is third – he won bronze in 2015 behind Lionel Messi and Cristiano Ronaldo!

12

West Ham had a £12 million bid rejected for an 18-year-old Neymar back in 2010!

65+

He's scored over 65 goals for Brazil and is closing in on becoming his country's all-time top goalscorer. He's also in the top five for matches played!

68

At the end of 2020-21, Neymar had been involved in a goal every 68 minutes in Ligue 1 since joining PSG!

14,000

Around 14,000 fans signed a petition for him to feature for Brazil at the 2010 World Cup when he was just 18 years old, but Dunga decided to leave him out of the squad completely. Unlucky, Ney!

FIFA SKILLS

SHOWBOATING
Use these to really show off against your opponent!

QUICK BALL ROLLS ★★★★

On page 14 we already told you how to add a simple Ball Roll to your game, but here's how to speed things up a bit! MATCH can't get enough of this awesome skill move!

HOLD: R Stick Down

PERFECT PLAYER
EDEN HAZARD

ELASTICO ★★★★★

It's fair to say that Marcus Rashford loves busting out this move for Manchester United and England, so he's a really good player to practise it with!

ROTATE: R Stick 180°   **OR ROTATE:** R Stick 180°

PERFECT PLAYER
MARCUS RASHFORD

RAINBOW ★★★★★

MATCH reckons this is one of the coolest flicks to pull off on FIFA and it's a great way of setting yourself up for an epic volley! Get practising ASAP!

FLICK: R Stick Down, R Stick Up + R Stick Up

PERFECT PLAYER
JAMES RODRIGUEZ

SOMBRERO FLICK ★★★★★

Nobody makes defenders look silly more often than Brazil trick machine Neymar, which is why he's one of the best players to use if you're looking to pull off this epic move!

FLICK: (While standing) R Stick Up, R Stick Up + R Stick Down

PERFECT PLAYER
NEYMAR

WORDSEARCH

Find 30 jaw-dropping skill moves in the giant grid below!

```
V S M V                                                           A H Y D
X H C E                                                           U S W Z
X V H L                                                           H V N C
T J H G                                                           U F Q W
Y G W G                                                           M O V H

R J C U V F H O Y L N Q R L C I E G S E Z H C V F D N Z S A
T V B J U S O L J Z Y Z P F A V B F L I P - F L A P B M U K
E Q M F U A T M Y D S D K M N J F U P G H K P N G B O F F C
Z G A F L Z M O A A G B N K F C J D X I M B G Z I A B B I A
Z V I V A C D A P C S S L M C A K V I B Y M E R T X N P O B
A C K F B F Y E P U Q V D A Z A L E W N M G Z N W H O O I G
H J H V J A X U C P K F E R A S K V L Q A M S G B H R Q B A
X W R L W S U O A U K X R A B U I N F A Z V V R L O U D E R
B Q Y M P Q P V D R S B T B S D X D U I S K L L H M O D W D
D A G I O S I J G E O H X O Y S L V E C Y T A L D X E F T U
F P N P U F N S G A A U W N L B C A T B K B I A O B T C X T
P X E C G K X N Y I R O N A N Y Y S T Y L L F C R R X D S M
X A O R X Z A K K S R V B D P X A Y K Y N W E C O W L F Y O
Q H V J T H X W W C V H A U T Z T Y Z L U O S B R P O L V D
K N S C C B C U O N I Y A X K H N C O E K L T G A D M R A T
R E S E Z B Q V T X H L J U N H E Y U R N O X M I L U O N B
H Y N S O E E H N D Q Y F O O F S W Z T T D D V S V L U W K
M A Y D C N P Y I R N M K O B J A E O U L T W I K I W L R P
L R O M O O K P E Z L X Y Q R V S S A R V N T G V V A E S N
H O G V S O R F F X W S F S O E Q R H L L O W A K Q O T N X
J Z A T N G Y P A A K X J S N I R R E T D D H C C K J T R I
J J C Z T D O O I C S T M H N F M B B V D R A E R R V E U R
I N E U B O K G I O B V E O P H T B M L O B I I L B M W T O
G J X Y B M L L D C N M C T C C L V D O L P B B M X F A F N
F X I D L A F K T N B K M I L X L N R L S E E Y B I A K F A
Y U N V C T I H E B R V I G V F W M U G A S O T Q L K A Y L
I T X K S R T E E Z Q Z G C T N J P A A H C K Z S W E W U D
N P Q E G P C Y L U D K C I K R O S S I C S R N M U S A R O
G V H O W W P V K A M G Z O K A V N P L W P I O P S H K C C
H C A F W K R R F C J A C O J V F Y U C D Q L G Q B O A B H
E R C C P R Z N A V F N Y J M J J G E M T U N H M U T W O O
B J C T R E P O D A N R O T L E W A C W S M M E D S E Z L P
J A E J E T T V K C I L F W O B N I A R U C S M R C V T D P
E O E O Q T N R B M D U D M M E C K C E J G X V Y O V V A J
K M S C J G Z Y F R B U E D L V F Y G P U Z K B O I B K A H
```

Around The World	**Dummy**	**Hocus Pocus**	**Pullback V**	**Scorpion Kick**
Ball Hop	**El Tornado**	**Juggle**	**Rabona**	**Seal Dribble**
Ball Roll	**Elastico**	**Knuckleball**	**Rainbow Flick**	**Sombrero Flick**
Chest Flick	**Fake Shot**	**La Croqueta**	**Ronaldo Chop**	**Spin**
Cruyff Turn	**Feint**	**Lane Change**	**Roulette**	**Stepover**
Drag Back	**Flip-Flap**	**Nutmeg**	**Scissor Kick**	**Waka Waka**

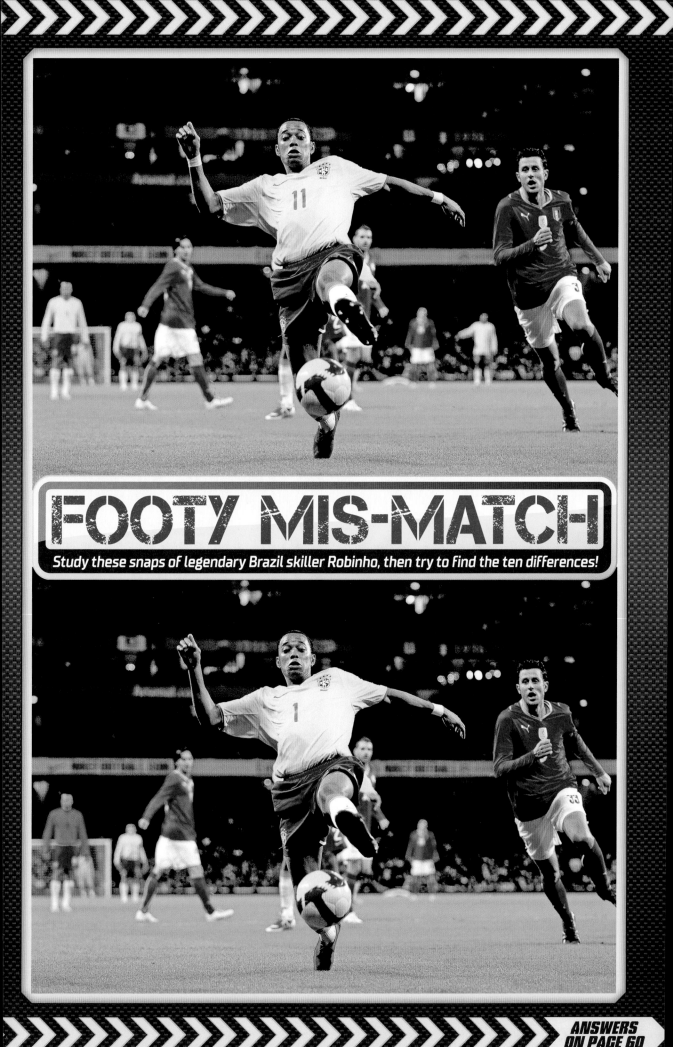

FOOTY MIS-MATCH

Study these snaps of legendary Brazil skiller Robinho, then try to find the ten differences!

ANSWERS ON PAGE 60

PICK YOUR TOP 5 WOMEN SKILLERS!

DEBINHA
North Carolina Courage & Brazil

JI SO-YUN
Chelsea & South Korea

AMEL MAJRI
Lyon & France

For the chance to win this absolutely mind-blowing gaming bundle, just write down your five favourite women skillers on the football planet, fill out your contact details and email a photograph of this page to: **match.magazine@kelsey.co.uk** Closing date: January 31, 2022. Come on, what are you waiting for?

1.

2.

3.

4.

5.

NAME:

DATE OF BIRTH:

ADDRESS:

MOBILE:

EMAIL:

Wordfit — P20

Saint-Maximin Quiz — P21

1. Younger; 2. False; 3. Nice;
4. Sheffield United; 5. True.

Spot The Ball — P21

I12.

The Nickname Game — P31

1. Douglas Costa - B. Flash;
2. Neymar - E. The Gem;
3. Hakim Ziyech - F. The Wizard;
4. Lionel Messi - D. The Flea;
5. Angel Di Maria - C. Noodle;
6. Martin Odegaard - A. The King.

Odd One Out — P31

Jadon Sancho has never played in Spain's La Liga.

Face In The Crowd — P45

Crossword — P30

Brain-Buster — P44

1. False; 2. Sao Paulo;
3. Leicester; 4. More than 100;
5. Benfica; 6. Ivory Coast; 7. 16 years old; 8. Cristiano Ronaldo;
9. Less than £30 million; 10. Nike.

Wordsearch — P56

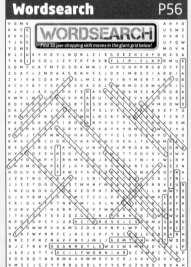

Footy Mis-Match — P57